Time-Savers for Teachers

WRITING NON-FICTION YEARS 3-4

W
FRANKLIN WATTS
LONDON•SYDNEY

How to use this book

This book provides a range of worksheets suitable for children in Years 3 and 4 of primary school. The worksheets are grouped into sections which correspond to the text types specified in the National Literacy Strategy. The contents are equally relevant to the Scottish 5-14 Guidelines, and the curricula for the Republic and Northern Ireland.

Each section starts with an introduction which sets out the *key features* of the relevant text type, followed by sample *annotated text* and a *model text* for the children. The worksheets have been carefully selected to cater for *different* levels of ability. At the end of each section, text frames and scaffolds provide guidance for *writing* assignments. There is also a *skills checklist* to enable you to keep track of individual children's progress. There is a final checklist of the National Literacy Strategy objectives covered in the book on page 96. All teacher-pages have a vertical stripe down the side of the page.

All the worksheets are photocopiable.

This edition first published in 2004

Franklin Watts
338 Euston Road, London NW1 3BH

Contributors: John Barwick, Sharon Dalgleish, Tanya Dalgleish, Karen Dobbie, Ann Doherty, Michael Faye, Angela Lloyd, Sharon Shapiro
Adapted by Brenda Stones
Educational advisers: Sarah St John, Jo Owston

ISBN 978 0 7496 5808 3

Printed in Dubai

Franklin Watts is a division of Hachette Children's Books.

Contents

Recount texts

Recounts can be personal, factual, or imaginative, or a combination of these: e.g. A Letter Home is imaginative and factual, while The Trip to the Zoo is imaginative and personal.

Features	Personal recount	Factual recount	Imaginative recount
Audience	Child or adult	Child or adult	Child or adult
Tense	Past tense	Past tense	Past tense
Language	Often focuses on adding personal and emotive responses.	The focus is on using evaluative language (e.g. importance, significance, influence, achievement).	Often includes imagined personal responses.
First or third person	Written in first person using personal pronouns (I, we).	Written in third person using pronouns (he, she, they). It may be written in the passive voice.	Written in the first person (I, we).
Addition of details	Interesting ideas may be chosen to add some humour.	Precise re-telling assists readers to accurately reconstruct what happened. Appropriate explanations and justifications may be included. Sometimes in an experiment the outcome of the activity is explained.	Imaginative details may be added to the tale that has been written in a realistic setting.
Series of events	Sequenced details of who, what, when, where and why (sometimes) are included.	Precise details of time, place and manner are added.	Sequenced details of who, what, when and where are included.

Sample annotated text

 Letter Home

Sydney Cove
New South Wales
Great South Land
27th January, 1788

Dear Mother and Father,

**Orientation —
who, where,
when, how, what**

We are off the ship at last! I am writing you this letter from the **new colony of New South Wales**. All nine ships in the **First Fleet arrived** here **safely yesterday**. Many of the sailors and officers **said** it was **a successful expedition** but we convicts thought it was dreadful.

In February **I** was loaded onto the transport ship, **Friendship**. The living quarters were very crowded, dirty and smelly. Three of us **had** to share a bunk! There were cockroaches, lice and rats! We had to wear leg irons all the time until four weeks later when Captain Arthur Phillip ordered them to be removed because of the **rough** seas and our **terrible** seasickness.

Series of events

Personal Comments

After we **left** Tenerife the sea became very calm and there was no wind. The ship **hardly** moved at all. When we **crossed** the equator the sailors had a ceremony thanking Poseidon (that's the god of the sea) for giving them a **safe** voyage.

When we left Cape Town on the 13th of November the seas became **rougher**, the winds **stronger** and the temperature **colder**. There was snow, sleet and thick fog. I was very scared! I thought the ship would be capsized with all hands lost in those freezing seas. The winds were called the **Roaring Forties and** helped push the fleet east across the Southern Ocean.

Day after day we would stare ahead to the east waiting for our first glimpse of the Great South Land. On the 5th of January Van Diemen's Land was sighted. Soon after this we turned north. **Finally** we **sailed** into a wide and shallow bay. **We were told** this was Botany Bay, discovered by Captain James Cook in 1770. Captain Phillip **decided** it was too swampy and the soil too sandy for farming so we left Botany Bay to sail further north.

We had sailed for only two hours **when** the fleet entered the most **beautiful** harbour in the world. There were many bays in this harbour that we could have weighed anchor in **but** Captain Phillip found a deep, sheltered little cove. He called it Sydney Cove. He and the officers went ashore to raise the flag.

Today we were taken ashore for the first time since leaving England. We have been unloading supplies and farm animals and clearing the bush all day. We convicts have to build houses and convict quarters, look after the cows and pigs, and farm vegetables and crops. I think it will be a very long time before another ship arrives from England with more supplies.

Re-orientation

I miss you terribly and hope you are all well. I often wonder what my life will be like in this strange new land.

Your loving son

Michael

PS My letter may not reach you for more than a year and I may well be a man of 18 by the time you read this.

Use of nouns and pronouns identifying people, places and things, e.g. I, we, First Fleet, Friendship, New South Wales

Use of noun groups to build up a description, e.g. the new colony of New South Wales

Use of past tense, e.g. left, had, sailed

Use of action verbs, e.g. arrived, crossed

Use of evaluative language, e.g. rougher, colder, stronger

Use of saying verbs, e.g. said, decided

Use of technical terms, e.g. the Roaring Forties

Use of connecting words, e.g. finally

Use of conjunctions, e.g. but, when, and

Use of adjectives, e.g. rough, terrible, beautiful, safe

Use of adverbs, e.g. safely, yesterday, hardly

Use of reported speech, e.g. We were told...

A Letter Home (part 1)

Sydney Cove
New South Wales
Great South Land
27th January, 1788

Dear Mother and Father,

We are off the ship at last! I am writing you this letter from the new colony of New South Wales. All nine ships in the First Fleet arrived here safely. Many of the sailors and officers said it was a successful expedition but we convicts thought it was dreadful.

In February I was loaded onto the transport ship, Friendship. The living quarters were very crowded, dirty and smelly. Three of us had to share a bunk! There were cockroaches, lice and rats! We had to wear leg irons all the time until four weeks later when Captain Arthur Phillip ordered them to be removed because of the rough seas and our terrible seasickness.

After we left Tenerife the sea became very calm and there was no wind. The ship hardly moved at all. When we crossed the equator the sailors had a ceremony thanking Poseidon (that's the god of the sea) for giving them a safe voyage.

A Letter Home (part 2)

When we left Cape Town on the 13th of November the seas became rougher, the winds stronger and the temperature colder. There was snow, sleet and thick fog. I was very scared! I thought the ship would be capsized with all hands lost in those freezing seas. The winds were called the Roaring Forties and helped push the fleet east across the Southern Ocean.

Day after day we would stare ahead to the east waiting for our first glimpse of the Great South Land. On the 5th of January Van Diemen's Land was sighted. Soon after this we turned north. Finally we sailed into a wide and shallow bay. We were told this was Botany Bay, discovered by Captain James Cook in 1770. Captain Phillip decided it was too swampy and the soil too sandy for farming so we left Botany Bay to sail further north.

We had sailed for only two hours when the fleet entered the most beautiful harbour in the world. There were many bays in this harbour that we could have weighed anchor in but Captain Phillip found a deep, sheltered little cove. He called it Sydney Cove. He and the officers went ashore to raise the flag.

Today we were taken ashore for the first time since leaving England. We have been unloading supplies and farm animals and clearing the bush all day. We convicts have to build houses and convict quarters, look after the cows and pigs, and farm vegetables and crops. I think it will be a very long time before another ship arrives from England with more supplies.

I miss you terribly and hope you are all well. I often wonder what my life will be like in this strange new land,

Your loving son
Michael

PS My letter may not reach you for more than a year and I may well be a man of 18 by the time you read this.

Biography

Name _____

Read 'A Letter Home'. Work with one or two friends to create an imaginary account of Michael's life. Discuss when and where he was born, his family life, the crime he committed and why he committed it. Jointly write a short recount – a biography – of Michael's life until his arrest. You may wish to describe his appearance and include a portrait drawing of him. Write your final version on the lines.

Dear Michael

Name _____

Read 'A Letter Home'. Imagine that you are Michael's mother or father. Write a reply to his letter recounting events that have happened in your life since he left England. You should remember to include an orientation (explain who, where, when, how or what), re-tell events in order and end with a re-orientation. Don't forget to use past tense verbs.

Revise, edit and proofread your draft, then write your final version below.

The Trip to the Zoo (part 1)

This is a telephone conversation between a grandmother and her grandaughter about the grandaughter's trip to the zoo.

Hello Grandma. How are you?

I'm fine, Kate, dear. Where did you go on Saturday?

To the zoo.

You are a lucky girl. What time did you leave?

Nine o'clock.

Who did you go with?

My mum and my dad.

That's lovely. Did you take your little sister too?

No.

No? Why?

Because she's too small. She can't walk yet.

Oh, what a pity. Couldn't you have taken her in the pushchair?

No. It was too far.

How did you get there?

We caught a bus and then a train and then a ferry.

What did you do at the zoo?

We walked and walked and walked all around the zoo and looked at all the animals.

What animals did you see?

First we watched the lions. They were tired. They were sleeping. But the tiger wasn't sleeping and he growled and growled really loud.

Did that frighten you?

No way, Grandma, he was in a big strong cage. And the giraffe was eating grass from a big tall basket.

Where did you go after the giraffe?

We went to see the elephant and the elephant lifted his trunk up over the fence and licked Dad's ice cream. He tried to get it back, but the elephant put it in his mouth and ate it up.

The Trip to the Zoo (part 2)

Oh, poor Daddy. And then what happened?

Then we went in the cable car and we could see all the pink birds in the big pond.

And after that, what did you do?

We went to see the koalas. The man gave them some food. Mum took a photo of them and then we rode on the train.

Where did the train go?

It went round and round and stopped at the station. Then we had lunch at the restaurant. I had saugage and chips and ice cream.

Sounds yummy. What did you do after lunch?

After lunch we went to see the dolphins.

What did the dolphins do?

They swam in the water and jumped through the hoop and made a big splash. My clothes got wet, but Mum said it didn't matter because it was sunny.

Did you see any other animals?

No because it was three o'clock and Dad said we had to go and catch the ferry. But at the gates we went to the zoo shop and looked at all the things.

What did you see in the shop?

Lots of things for people to buy – souvenirs Dad said they're called – so you can remember your trip.

Did you buy any souvenirs?

No way Grandma 'cause I didn't have any money. But Mum bought a T-shirt for Phoebe and some animal books and a video.

Nothing for me?

Oh, silly billy Grandma, Dad bought a surprise for you so I can't tell you that.

You're a bit of a trickster, aren't you? When did you get back home?

At five o'clock.

Did you have a good time?

Yes and when Phoebe is bigger I'm going to take her to the zoo, and you can come too Grandma.

Timeline

Read 'A Trip to the Zoo'. This conversation recounts some parts of the trip to the zoo. A recount begins with an orientation (which provides some background information) and then reconstructs the past events in chronological order. Reread the recount and locate each of the events. Create a timeline to clearly record the events in order.

DID DADDY CARRY YOU?

NOON   1 PM   2 PM   3 PM   4 PM

Write a letter

Name _____

The recount that you read is the transcript of a conversation. Recounts can also be written down. Imagine that you are Kate and write a letter to your grandmother telling her about the trip to the zoo. Use the information in the conversation and the timeline that you have created to write this letter. Work on rough paper and write the edited version in the space below.

Recount scaffold

Name _____

Orientation
This supplies the background information and answers these questions:

When? _____

_____

What? _____

_____

Where?_____

_____

Who? _____

Why? (not always included) _____

_____

Series of Events

List of events	Your response to each event	Order of events

Re-orientation

_____

_____

_____

_____

_____

Recount skills checklist

Name:				
Class:	Date/Level	Date/Level	Date/Level	Date/Level
PURPOSE				
Demonstrates understanding of the purpose of recounts.				
STRUCTURE				
Writes an orientation which includes the *when*, *who*, *what* and *where*.				
Sequences the series of events chronologically.				
Uses a re-orientation to round off the series of events.				
Adds personal responses and evaluative language to comment on the situation.			⌣	
TEXT ORGANISATION				
Plans for the writing of a recount.				
Writes events in the order that they occurred.				
Writes personal comments.				
Creates timelines, maps, flow charts and diagrams to add detail to recounts.				
Recognises the difference between spoken and written, personal, factual and imaginative recounts.				
Makes correct use of paragraphs.				
LANGUAGE FEATURES				
Uses nouns and pronouns to identify people, animals or things.				
Uses nouns and noun groups to build up descriptions.				
Uses action verbs to discuss events.				
Uses adjectives to add details.				
Uses adverbs and adverbial phrases to indicate place and time.				
Uses past tense to locate events in the speaker's time.				
Uses conjunctions to combine clauses.				
Uses connecting words to sequence events.				
Uses reported speech to explain events.				
Uses evaluative language in factual and personal recounts.				

LEVEL CODES   1 Consistently evident   2 Sometimes evident   3 Not evident

Instruction texts

Structure and features of instruction texts

PURPOSE

The main purpose of an instruction is to direct, inform or explain. An instruction explains how to do something.

TYPES OF INSTRUCTION

Instructions must serve a purpose and must be appropriate for an audience, such as a child or adult. Instructions may be spoken, written or visual, and can take place face to face, on the telephone or on the radio. These may involve physical activity, mental thought or emotional behaviour.

There are different types of instruction texts serving different purposes. Instructions can instruct how to do a particular activity, for example science experiments, stage directions, road safety rules, following an itinerary and recipes. Instructions can help people by teaching them what is appropriate behaviour, for example how to succeed. Instructions normally take the form of directions or instructions. Directions depend on someone with the knowledge having the skills to pass them on accurately, and will direct someone to a place. Instructions will methodically explain how to make or do something, how something works or how it is used. Examples would be instruction manuals or operating instructions.

Instruction texts communicate the rules, processes or stages for all the above activities. In addition, instructions can be part of a mixed text type such as a report on an experiment and can be found in letters, games, pamphlets, newspapers, magazines, television and on signs and maps where they carry the meaning of the text.

STRUCTURE OF INSTRUCTION TEXTS

In instruction texts the focus is on systematically explaining a logical sequence of actions or steps. First you do this, then you do that. Each event or step must be clearly and explicitly written so that the reader can carry out the same activity. For example, the text may include the sequence of actions to be followed to reach a required location. Texts are usually written in the present tense and in general terms. This enables any person to use them.

These texts are often accompanied by diagrams, graphs, charts and pictures which need: to be read; the technical language understood; and the syntax, which is often more formal, abstract and less predictable than that found in narratives, deciphered.

Teachers should select texts for pupils to read that are clearly organised, with headings and subheadings that indicate different content. These texts need to be examined to see if there is sufficient contextual support for the technical vocabulary to support the reader. Teachers need to provide scaffolding strategies in order to assist pupils to access information and meaning in the texts.

Each type of instruction text will have a standard format according to its purpose. Directions, rules and spoken instructions may have a structure that is slightly different from one explaining how to make something. Written steps can consist of a map with steps that are coded and use arrows, symbols or compass points. Alternatively the steps can be written in note form with illustrations, diagrams, cartoons, flow charts and photos clarifying the meaning. Other text types, for example descriptions and explanations, can be found within these texts.

The structure usually consists of three stages:

1 An introductory statement that gives the heading, the goal or the aim of the activity and states what the instruction is aiming to achieve. Sometimes the goal is indicated in the main heading for example, 'Building a Model of a Dinosaur'. This may be aided by a diagram or map.

2 The listing of materials or equipment to be used.

3 The method or sequence of steps written in the order in which they should be completed.

Instructions focus on people and things in general terms, referring to the reader in general terms as 'you'. They provide specific descriptions of things, such as amounts of ingredients or size and shape of equipment. Specific information is included about how, when and where actions are to be carried out, for example quickly, until cooked through (how), after the top has dried (when), in a large dish (where).

Here are a few variations of the above:

- Recipes generally are divided into ingredients and method.
- Instructions for games usually include how to play, rules of the game, method of scoring and number of players.
- Scientific experiments usually include the purpose of the experiment, equipment, observations and conclusion.

Each stage plays a role in explaining what we need or what precisely we have to do next. Each step is ordered and sometimes numbered. Some instructions have an optional stage that explains reasons for steps and will offer alternative methods. The text may include comments or warnings about dangerous aspects and consequences, or describe enjoyable aspects of the task. Hints or warnings can be added at different points, for example 'Take care when picking up the sharp point'.

LANGUAGE FEATURES OF INSTRUCTION TEXTS

- Nouns or noun groups are used in the listed materials or equipment, e.g. screws, nuts, bolts, screwdriver, wood.
- Often the name of an item is omitted instead of being constantly repeated and an ellipsis is used. The person following the instructions may not be referred to or may be referred to in a general way as 'one' or 'you'. There is little use of personal pronouns.
- Conjunctions are used to show chronological order, e.g. before, while, then, after, when.
- Action verbs start most sentences, in the imperative form, e.g. take, put, link.
- Short statements or commands are used, e.g. Pick them up.
- Adjectives add details relating to size, shape, colour and amount, e.g. Place the red cube there.
- Words related to direction and specific location are found, e.g. left, north, Jamison Street.
- Present tense is generally used.
- Vocabulary ranges from technical to everyday language according to the target audience.
- Emphasis is often given to important information by underlining it or writing in bold.
- Adverbs, prepositions and adverbial phrases add detailed information about how, where and when.
- Clear, simple, precise, but detailed, language is used.

Sample annotated text

TEXT ORGANISATION

TEXT ORGANISATION

LANGUAGE FEATURES

Snap Trap!

Goal or aim

*Here is a magic trick to trap **your** friends!*

Clear, precise but detailed language

Referred to in general terms, e.g. your

Materials or equipment

You'll need:

a crisp, **new** banknote or a piece of paper about the same size.

Use of present tense, e.g. hold, catch

Let's do it:

Chronological steps

1 First, **hold** the end of the note or paper in one hand.

2 **Then let it hang straight down.**

3 Now **bring** your other hand up to the middle of the note.

4 **Position your thumb** and index finger on each side of the note but don't touch it yet!

Use of action verbs, e.g. hold, bring

Use of short statements, e.g. Then let it hang straight down

5 **Let the note fall** then **catch** it between your thumb and index finger.

Diagrams

6 Now ask your friends to try to catch the note as you let it fall. They won't be able to!

7 **After** they have tried **a few times**, offer to help by telling them when you are going to let go. Say something like, 'One, two, three, drop!' They still won't be able to catch the magic note!

Use of commands, e.g. Position your thumb, Let the note fall

Use of conjunctions, e.g. after, before

Use of adverbial phrases, e.g. a few times

Explanation

How it works:

The note will always slip through the other **person's** fingers **before** their brain has time to send a message to the fingers to catch it.

Use of adjectives, e.g. person's, new

Use of causal connections, e.g. before

Snap Trap!

Here is a magic trick to trap your friends!

You'll need:

a crisp, new banknote or a piece of paper about the same size.

Let's do it:

1. First, hold the end of the note or paper in one hand.

2. Then let it hang straight down.

3. Now bring your other hand up to the middle of the note.

4. Position your thumb and index finger on each side of the note but don't touch it yet!

5. Let the note fall then catch it between your thumb and index finger.

6. Now ask your friends to try to catch the note as you let it fall. They won't be able to!

7. After they have tried a few times, offer to help by telling them when you are going to let go. Say something like, 'One, two, three, drop!' They still won't be able to catch the magic note!

How it works:

The note will always slip through the other person's fingers before their brain has time to send a message to the fingers to catch it.

Draw a diagram

Name _____

Read 'Snap Trap'. Create a series of diagrams to replace the instructions. Your diagrams should make the magic trick easy to understand and perform. Draft your diagrams, then show them to a partner.

Does your partner think they are easy to follow? Do they match the instructions? Have you left anything out? Is anything confusing? Answer any questions that your partner might ask about your diagrams.

Now make any changes needed and draw your final diagrams in the space below.

Identify the features

Read the instructions again. Find as many features as you can which identify this piece of writing as an instruction.

Write a list of all the features of an instruction text.

From Time-Savers for Teachers: Non-fiction Years 3-4. This page may be reproduced for classroom use.

21

How to Play Hopscotch

You will need

a flat pebble or a piece of wood

a hopscotch grid marked on the playground

Rules

1 Players must not step on the lines of the grid while hopping.

2 Players must not hop in a square which has a pebble in it.

3 Players are able to place two hands on the ground to balance themselves when picking up their pebble.

4 If a player's pebble lands on a line when they are aiming for a square, then it is a 'liner'. The player has another go. If the player's pebble lands outside the square they are aiming for, then it is the next player's turn.

How to play

1 Decide who will go first.

2 Throw your pebble from the base to the square marked 1.

3 Hop over the first square to the second.

4 Hop on all the squares in turn up to 7 and 8.

5 Turn around on 7 and 8 and hop back to 2.

6 Pick up your pebble from 1, while standing on 2, without putting your foot down.

7 Hop over 1 to base.

8 The player continues if this is done without a mistake.

9 Throw the pebble from the base onto the square marked 2.

10 Hop on the first square, then over the second square to the third.

11 Continue playing in this way, throwing the pebble onto 3, 4 etc up to the highest number and back again to 1.

12 The player who reaches the first square again is the winner.

Grid games

Name _____

Work with a partner. Discuss how hopscotch could be played using the different grids. Now, write a set of simple instructions for one of them.

7	8	7	8
	6	6	
4	5	4	5
	3	3	
	2	2	
	1	1	

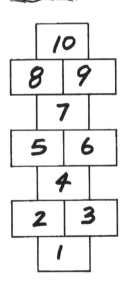

8		9
	7	
6	–	10
	5	
4		11
	3	
2		12
	1	

HOME
10
9
8
7
6
5
4
3
2
1

_____

_____

_____

_____

_____

_____

_____

Nutty Honey Flakes

Ingredients

40 g butter

1 dessertspoon sugar

2 tablespoons honey

60 g unsalted peanuts

3 cups cornflakes

WE'RE NUTTY FLAKES.

Method

1   Preheat oven to 200°C.

2   Put honey, sugar and butter into a small saucepan. Stir over low heat until butter has melted.

3   Combine peanuts and cornflakes in a bowl. Pour in butter and honey syrup mixture.

4   Mix well until peanuts and cornflakes are coated in syrup.

5   Lay out patty cases in patty cake tins. Spoon 1 tablespoon of mixture into each patty case.

6   Bake for 8 minutes. Remove from oven and leave to stand until cool and syrup has set.

Makes about 20.

What do I do next?

Name _____

Read the recipe 'Nutty Honey Flakes'.

Create a flow diagram to show the steps in the recipe.

A FLOW DIAGRAM

Nouns, verbs and adverbs

Name _____

Look carefully at the word classes in the recipe 'Nutty Honey Flakes'
and complete the table.

Verbs	Nouns	Adverbial phrases (how, when or where)
Preheat	oven	to 200°C
Put	honey, sugar and butter	into a small saucepan

Talk with a partner about your findings.

How can I do that?

Write an instruction for a task with which you are familiar, for example washing the dishes or making a peanut butter sandwich. Think about the features of an instruction before you begin.

YOU NEED A KNIFE FOR SPREADING AND A SPOON FOR EATING !!

How to Get to the Shops

A: Peter, can you go to the shops for me please? I need a few things for lunch.

P: Sure, Aunty Angela.

A: Sit down here and I'll tell you what to do. You'll have to listen carefully and follow my directions. Here's a map I've drawn for you.

P: OK.

A: First, I want you to go to the fruit shop. I need two avocados and an apple.

P: How do I get to the fruit shop?

A: It's in Mercer Street, right next to the bank. Walk straight up Wolseley Road until you get to the lights. Push the button for the lights – make sure you wait until it says walk. Cross the road and walk up the street. The fruit market is the second shop from the end.

P: Oh yeah. I know where that is. There's a record shop on the other side of it.

A: That's right. From there I want you to go to the bakery in Park Street. Walk out of the fruit shop. Keep walking up the street, past the record store. Frederick Street is the next street on your left. Turn left down there and cross over Hill Street. Keep walking until you get to Park Street. Turn left into Park Street. The baker is just on the corner. Get a loaf of bread and four meat pies.

P: Yum!

A: I also need some stamps. You can buy them at the post office in Conrack Street. Do you remember how to get up to Conrack Street?

P: Sort of. I know where it is.

A: Go back out of the bakery, and wait at the lights to cross Frederick Street. Walk straight up Park Street towards the park. Conrack Street is the next street that you come to. Turn right, and the post office is about the fourth one down, next to the newsagent. Is it clear so far?

P: Easy!

A: To get home, just turn right into Mercer Street and walk right along until you get to Wolseley Road. Cross at the lights, remember! From there it's a straight walk home.

P: I'm on my way.

> WELL, I REMEMBERED HOW TO GET HERE.... BUT WHAT DID SHE WANT?

Let me write that down

Name _____

Peter's aunt told him how to reach the shops. While she spoke, Peter made a list of the most important steps in the directions. On the lines below, write the notes that Peter might have made.

_____

_____

_____

_____

_____

_____

_____

This is the map that Peter's aunt gave him. On the map, mark the route that Peter took. Use your notes to help you.

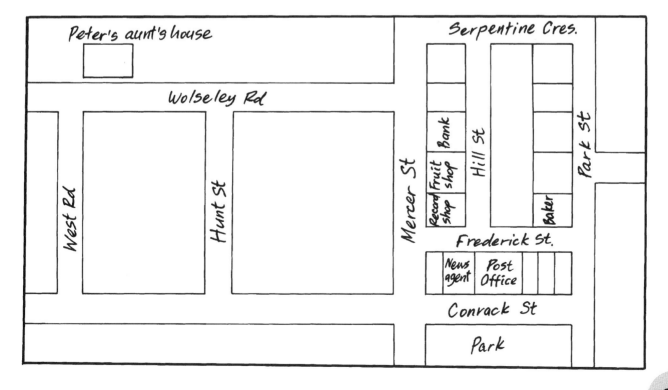

Find another way

Name _____

Peter had to walk to three different places to buy things for his aunt. He had to go to:
- the fruit shop in Mercer Street
- the baker in Park Street
- the post office in Conrack Street.

Choose one of these places and write a new set of directions to tell how to get there from Peter's aunt's house. Write your directions on the lines below.

_____

_____

_____

_____

_____

_____

_____

Listen carefully

Read the directions you wrote in the previous activity to a partner. As you read, your partner must use a coloured pencil to mark the route on the map in his or her workbook. Did your partner follow your directions exactly? Did your partner think that your directions were clear? Now swap roles. Listen as your partner reads his or her directions. Mark the route on the map.

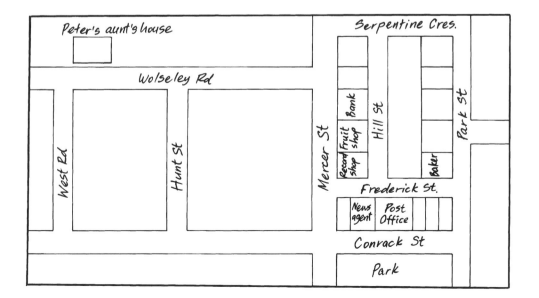

Where's the treasure?

Name _____

In the space below, create a map of the classroom.
Hide a treasure in the classroom and mark the hiding place on the map.

Write some directions which will help someone find the treasure.
You'll need to choose a starting place on the map first.

_____

_____

_____

_____

_____

_____

_____

_____

_____

Read your directions to a partner – but don't show them the map just yet! Did they find the treasure? How effective were your directions? How can they be improved?

Instruction scaffold

Use this sheet to plan an instruction text on a topic of your choice.

Name _____

Instruction scaffold

Introductory statement giving the aim or goal
This may be a title or an introductory paragraph.

_____

_____

Material needed for completing the instruction
This can take the form of a list, or a paragraph, or may be omitted from some instructions.

_____

_____

Action plan
This is a sequence of steps in the correct order. The sequence can be numbered as first, second, third etc. or the words *now*, *next* and *after this* can be used. Steps generally begin with a command, for example *fold* or *cross*.

Step 1 _____

_____

Step 2 _____

_____

Step 3 _____

_____

Step 4 _____

_____

Step 5 _____

_____

Evaluation _____

_____

Any further action to be taken? _____

_____

DIAGRAM

Instruction skills checklist

Name:				
Class:	Date/Level	Date/Level	Date/Level	Date/Level
PURPOSE				
Demonstrates understanding of the purpose of instructions.				
STRUCTURE				
Writes an opening statement, goal or aim.				
Lists required materials or equipment.				
Orders a series of steps chronologically.				
Uses diagrams and headings to clarify instructions.				
Recognises different types of instruction texts.				
TEXT ORGANISATION				
Plans for instruction writing.				
Writes a clear sequence of events.				
Varies the amount of detail and content, depending on the target audience.				
Writes each step on a new line.				
Uses visual representations to clarify directions or instructions.				
LANGUAGE FEATURES				
Uses clear, precise, but detailed language.				
Uses nouns and noun groups.				
Uses action verbs to start sentences.				
Uses adjectives to add details.				
Uses adverbs and adverbial phrases to tell *how*, *where* and *when*.				
Uses present tense consistently.				
Uses conjunctions for time sequences.				

LEVEL CODES   1 Consistently evident   2 Sometimes evident   3 Not evident

Report texts

Structure and features of report texts

PURPOSE

Reports are generally used to organise and store factual information.

TYPES OF REPORT

Reports are generally written to cover the areas of natural science, technology and social science. Financial experts write reports on matters to do with the economy, geologists write reports for purposes of development and conservation, and medical researchers write reports for the information of other doctors and the public.

Reports have a variety of patterns and contain various types of information. They can classify information into different categories or examine the components and various aspects of an object. They involve pupils in developing the skills of naming, generalising, describing, defining, analysing, organising, comparing and contrasting.

Reports can involve a great deal of research. When writing reports, pupils will need to find suitable resources and develop research skills. They will need to read several sources to confirm statements or generalisations. Some topics will involve the development of understanding and usage of technical terminology. Pupils will also need to develop the skills to read the contents page, use the index and glossary, and take notes in a structured way. A scaffold consisting of a set of questions can be used to assist pupils when taking notes.

Reports can be presented orally or in a written form. Oral presentations can be used to present a lecture on a subject, or to give information on topics, such as scientific, manufactured or natural phenomena. Pupils should support these talks with models or charts in order to clarify information, and to ease and assist with the presentation of the great amount of content.

Written reports should be clear, interesting and of a good quality. The writer's voice should come through as an interested person who has developed some expertise and should not be too personal. Teachers will need to create opportunities to model the planning of a report using headings and note-taking. Pupils should be taught paragraphing skills, how to write topic sentences and how to elaborate giving further details and examples. For longer reports, pupils can make use of headings, subheadings, diagrams, captions and an index to help organise their notes. Teachers should also model correct acknowledgments, bibliographies, reference lists and citing of references. Examples of written reports appear in textbooks, lectures, research assignments and reference articles.

STRUCTURE OF REPORT TEXTS

In reports, the major focus is on describing a class of objects rather than discussing a sequence of activities or actions.

The structure includes:
- a general opening statement or classification
- a description consisting of a series of paragraphs
- a conclusion or a general rounding off statement
- visual elements in the form of diagrams or charts.

Introduction

In the introduction, the opening statement or classification explains the subject of the report. This may include a definition, classification or a short description. Sometimes the particular aspect being discussed may be stated.

Series of paragraphs

The introduction is followed by a series of paragraphs describing facts about various aspects and features of the subject. These facts should be divided into various topics, each grouped together in their own paragraphs. Each paragraph begins with a topic sentence and is then elaborated on by adding characteristics, details and facts about the topic, for example for a report on an animal, after the introduction the next paragraph may describe its appearance. This could be followed by a paragraph describing the habitat and the next paragraph could discuss the reproduction of the animal. A final paragraph before the concluding statement could contrast and compare different types.

Concluding paragraph

Reports frequently don't have a conclusion although sometimes a general statement rounds off the report. Concept maps, diagrams or tree diagrams will add additional information in a visual form.

LANGUAGE FEATURES OF REPORT TEXTS

- Use of a formal, accurate and objective style to deal with the facts. Personal opinions and comments are not added.
- Most reports use language economically. There are no irrelevant adjectives, adverbs, similes and metaphors.
- Generally written in third person.
- Use of noun groups to build up descriptions.
- Use of action verbs to describe behaviour, e.g. jump, devour, flee.
- Use of timeless present tense, e.g. are, thrive.
- Use of relating verbs to link features, e.g. is, are, has, have.

A cartoon *is* a drawing intended to influence public opinion.
- Use of technical and scientific language, e.g. species of animal.
- Use of paragraphs to organise information with the topic repeatedly named in subsequent paragraphs as the focus of the clause.
- Use of comparative adjectives; and defining and classifying adjectives, e.g. large, larger, largest; are called, are similar to, are stronger than, can be grouped.
- Use of factual and precise descriptive adjectives to give details about appearance, function and components, e.g. The twelve molar teeth in humans are used to grind food.
- Clauses are combined in different ways, e.g. If we removed all the trees from the area it would change the ecosystem for ever.
- Use of prepositions in phrases telling *where*, *when* and *how*.
- Use of time connectives.
- Limited use of personal pronouns.

Bananas (part 1)

A banana is a popular tropical fruit. There are more than 300 kinds of banana.

BANANAS are long and slightly curved and may grow up to twenty centimetres long. They are ripe when the skin turns yellow with some brown spots and the pulp is creamy and starting to soften.

BANANA PLANTS, or stools, look like palms. They can grow from three to nine metres high. Overlapping leaf stalks growing in layers grow up from an underground stem. Large leaves are at the end of each stalk. A flower shoot grows up through the centre of the hollow trunk. It bends towards the ground as it grows bigger and heavier. Bell-shaped buds form at the end of the flower shoots. These are surrounded by purple leaves called bracts. As the bracts peel back they expose yellowish flowers which soon grow into bananas. The bananas grow in clusters called hands and each banana is a 'finger'. It may take between twelve and eighteen months for a mature banana stool to produce ripe bananas.

Bananas (part 2)

BANANAS ARE GROWN

throughout the tropics, mainly in warm lowland areas. Bananas need to grow above the frost level and away from colder conditions. Central America and the West Indies export large quantities of bananas to North America and Europe.

HISTORIANS BELIEVE

bananas were among the first plants to be cultivated by people for food. The name 'banana' comes from Africa.

BANANAS CONTAIN mainly

water as well as large amounts of carbohydrate and vitamins A, B and C. Bananas are grown for fibre-making and ornamental reasons. However, most people enjoy them in cakes, pies, with ice cream as a banana split, in milkshakes, barbecued, frittered or instantly peeled as a healthy snack.

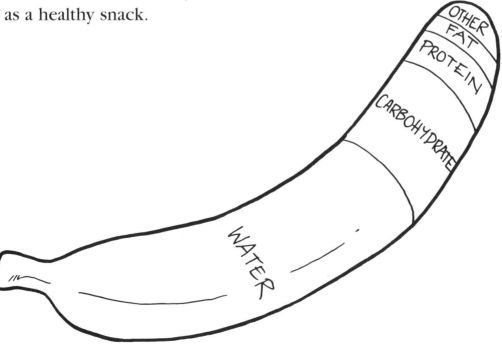

Sample annotated text

TEXT ORGANISATION

B à ná nà s

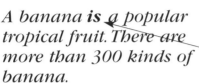

LANGUAGE FEATURES

*A banana **is** a popular tropical fruit. There are more than 300 kinds of banana.*

General opening statement or classification

BANANAS are long and slightly curved and may **grow** up to twenty centimetres long. They are ripe when the skin turns yellow with some brown spots and the pulp is creamy and starting to soften.

Description

BANANA PLANTS, or **stools**, look like palms. They can grow from three to nine metres high.

Appearance

Overlapping leaf stalks growing in layers grow up from an underground stem. Large leaves are at the end of each stalk. **A flower shoot** grows up

through the centre of the hollow trunk. It **bends** towards the ground as

Composition

it **grows bigger** and heavier. **Bell-shaped** buds form at the end of the flower shoots. These are surrounded by purple leaves called bracts. As the **bracts** peel back they expose yellowish flowers which soon grow into bananas. The bananas grow in

Rounding off statement

clusters called hands and each banana is a 'finger'. It may take between twelve and eighteen months for a mature banana stool to produce ripe bananas.

BANANA ARE GROWN

Location

throughout the tropics, mainly in

warm lowland areas. Bananas need to grow above the frost level and away from colder conditions. Central America and the West Indies export large quantities of bananas to North America and Europe.

HISTORIANS BELIEVE

bananas were among the first plants to be cultivated by people for food. The name 'banana' comes from Africa.

BANANAS CONTAIN

mainly water as well as large amounts of carbohydrate and vitamins A, B and C. Bananas are grown for fibre-making and ornamental reasons. However, most people enjoy them in cakes, pies, with ice cream as a banana split, in milkshakes, barbecued, frittered or instantly peeled as a healthy snack.

Paragraphs used to organise information

Written in third person

Use of present tense, e.g. are, is, grow

Use of technical and scientific language, e.g. stools, bracts

Use of noun groups to build descriptions, e.g. A flower shoot... through the centre of the hollow trunk

Use of action verbs, e.g. grows, bends

Use of comparatives, e.g. bigger

Use of precise descriptive adjectives, e.g. bell-shaped, overlapping leaf

Use of 'banana' as a focus of topic sentence for each paragraph

OTHER
FAT
PROTEIN
CARBOHYDRATE
WATER

Diagram of composition

Find the structure

A report often begins with a classification or a definition for the topic. For example, a report about mosquitoes may begin with a statement telling the reader that a mosquito is a small flying insect.

Read 'Bananas'. What is the general opening statement in this report?

_____

_____

_____

_____

In reports, information about the topic is organised into paragraphs.
Each paragraph introduces a new aspect of information.

After the introduction there are five paragraphs in this report.
What is the main idea in each paragraph?

1 _____

2 _____

3 _____

4 _____

5 _____

TODAY'S FRUIT OF STUDY
IS THE POTATO.

39

Welcome to Sandy Cove

Welcome to Sandy Cove – a fully patrolled beach with excellent facilities for all to enjoy.

The water temperature today is a refreshing 21°C. A light breeze is blowing from a north-easterly direction.

Swimmers should stay between the red and yellow flags as there is a strong undercurrent to the south of the swimming area. Board and jetski riders are requested not to enter this area between the flags.

There is a well-stocked kiosk by the children's playground. It sells ice cream, drinks, sandwiches, pies and sausage rolls. A range of sun-screen products is also for sale at the kiosk. The kiosk opens at 10.30 am and closes at 4 pm.

Our lifesavers will be on patrol until 5 pm today.

Enjoy your time at Sandy Cove!

Let's talk about it

Name _____

Read 'Welcome to Sandy Cove'. Have you heard announcements such as this at a beach, park or other public place? Who usually makes the announcements? Who is the audience? Why are these announcements made? Talk about it with a partner, then write your conclusions on the lines.

_____

_____

_____

_____

_____

What's it all about?

This announcement gives information to the listener. It is a non-chronological report. What is the opening statement in this announcement?

_____

_____

After the opening statement, reports give a series of facts about the topic. In the space below, list the facts given in the announcement.

_____

_____

_____

_____

Noun groups

On the lines below, list all the words in the Sandy Cove announcement that name and describe people, places or things. Remember – they can be nouns, noun groups or pronouns.

_____

_____

_____

_____

_____

Whales (part 1)

Whales are mammals which spend their entire life in the water. While a lot of other mammals are able to swim, there are very few which actually live in the water, but whales do. They breathe using lungs and give birth to live babies which feed on their mother's milk.

There are two distinct groups of whales – whales which have teeth and whales which don't have teeth. The whales which have teeth, such as the

sperm whale and killer whale, feed on squid and fish. The killer whale often eats other marine mammals, such as dolphins and seals. The whales which don't have teeth, such as the blue and fin whales, have mouths full of huge, hanging, fringed plates instead of teeth. These plates, or baleen, are edged with bristles and filter small animals and plankton from the water. Baleen whales eat by taking in water and then pushing it out through the bristles. The plankton and other small

animals get trapped by the bristles and are then swallowed. The blue whale, the largest baleen whale, can eat up to 8 tonnes of food per day.

Like fish, whales are streamlined for swimming, but they swim by moving their tail flukes up and down rather than from side to side. Instead of fins, whales have flippers at the front which they use for steering. Unlike fish which have scales, whales have very smooth, oily skin.

All mammals need air to survive. Whales have lungs and take air in through their nostrils, the single or double blowhole found at the top of their head. While they can hold their breath for a long time, sometimes up to an hour, they have to surface to breathe. When they do resurface, they push out the warm air from deep inside their body, which condenses into steam when it meets the cooler outside air. All whales make a blow like this as they breathe out. In the larger whales, this blow can reach up to ten metres high.

Whales mate like other mammals, and give birth to a live calf in the water, between nine months and a year

Whales (part 2)

later. As soon as it is born, the calf must get to the surface to breathe. The calf then stays close to the mother's side. It feeds on its mother's milk for many more months as it learns to swim and dive. At the end of its first year the calf may measure up to eight metres long.

Like humans, whales have five main senses but their hearing is particularly sensitive. Whales can hear the sounds of other whales, sea creatures and boats from far away. They send out sounds through their blowhole, and judge the distance of the other creature from the returning echo. Whales can keep in touch with one another by making lots of different noises such as thumps, squeaks and clicks.

Occasionally, whales get stranded on parts of the coast. Sometimes it involves one or two whales. At other times it involves a much larger number of whales. Experts are unsure why this happens but have a number of theories to explain it.

They think that whales become stranded because of sickness, old age or when they are injured. Another theory suggests that they lose their way due to bad weather, or they may be confused by the noise of large boats or by water pollution. Others think that whales may get trapped by a receding tide. When other members of the pod come to help, they too get stranded. Huge operations have been launched to try and help these whales back to the ocean.

Listen for the facts

Name _____

Listen carefully while your teacher reads the report 'Whales'. Record in the space below three or more interesting facts that you heard about whales.

_____

_____

_____

_____

Find the structure

The report begins with a general classification of whales. Each paragraph then describes something different about whales.

What is the general classification of the report?

_____

_____

What is the main idea in each of the next six paragraphs?

1 _____

2 _____

3 _____

4 _____

5 _____

6 _____

SO MUCH FOR OUR CHANCE TO BE ALONE !!

Just the facts

Name _____

The report 'Whales' gives you a lot of factual information. Work with a partner.
In the chart below record at least two facts for each paragraph.

General classification
Food and eating
How whales move
How whales breathe
Reproduction
Communication
Why whales get stranded

Brainstorming

Name

Use this sheet to brainstorm a topic to research.

Topic:

What I already know	What I would like to find out

Resources I will use

Taking notes

Name _____

Complete this sheet to research your chosen topic, using an information book.

Research topic
_____
_____

Key words to search
_____
_____

Resource
Title _____
Author _____
Publisher _____

Main points
_____
_____
_____
_____
_____
_____
_____
_____
_____

Diagram

Report scaffold

Name _____

Use this sheet to plan and write an information report.

Topic _____

General opening statement
_____
_____
_____

Series of paragraphs about the topic

Topic sentence _____
List of points _____
_____
_____
_____

Topic sentence _____
List of points _____
_____
_____
_____

Topic sentence _____
List of points _____
_____
_____
_____

Topic sentence _____
List of points _____
_____
_____
_____

Concluding paragraph or final sentence
_____
_____
_____
_____

Report skills checklist

Name:				
Class:	Date/Level	Date/Level	Date/Level	Date/Level
PURPOSE				
Understands the purpose of reports.				
STRUCTURE				
Writes a clear opening statement.				
Able to sequence a series of paragraphs, adding details.				
Writes a concluding statement or paragraph.				
Able to recognise different types of information reports.				
TEXT ORGANISATION				
Develops a well-sequenced plan for report writing.				
Able to research to find information suitable for headings.				
Developing sound note-taking skills.				
Writes paragraphs that have topic sentences and supporting details.				
Writes paragraphs that focus on specific areas of content.				
Lists detailed resources.				
LANGUAGE FEATURES				
Logically sequences facts using time connectives.				
Uses general nouns rather than specific nouns.				
Uses action verbs.				
Writes in present tense.				
Uses noun groups to build up descriptions.				
Uses language economically.				
Writes using third person.				
Uses technical and scientific language.				

LEVEL CODES   1 Consistently evident   2 Sometimes evident   3 Not evident

Explanation texts

Structure and features of explanation texts

PURPOSE

An explanation tells how and why something in the world happens. It is about actions rather than about things. Explanations play a valuable role in building and storing our knowledge. They are a central part of scientific writing and expressing scientific expertise.

TYPES OF EXPLANATION

When writing explanations, we establish that the phenomenon exists and then explain why or how this came about. The writer needs a great deal of content knowledge before beginning the explanation.

There are two basic types of explanations. The first type explains an occurrence or how something works. This may be mechanical when it explains how a kettle boils water, technological when it explains how a television works, and natural when describing how avalanches occur. The second type explains why things happen, for example why objects expand and contract or why we have a water cycle.

Explanations are written in a variety of areas. Medical researchers write explanations about how medical problems develop, for other doctors, nurses and health workers. Weather forecasters explain weather patterns and changes for farmers, students and scientists. A biologist will describe how butterflies develop from cocoons for conservationists and students. This text type has links with science and technology topics where explanations of natural or non-natural phenomena are explored, for example how a television works, how the water cycle works, how clouds are formed and how sound moves through a variety of materials. It also has links with PSHE with explanations such as why we should eat a healthy diet.

Technical terms play an important role in explanation texts. A glossary of terms may be included in the back of the book or writers may write a definition of terms within the text.

It is important that pupils understand that explanations can be part of a larger text. It is quite usual to find explanations within a report to explain some aspects of the information. Explanations can be found as an integral part of an instruction text, the instruction explaining to the reader how to do something and the explanation detailing how it works.

STRUCTURE OF EXPLANATION TEXTS

Explanations have the following structure:
- title
- general statement introducing or identifying the phenomenon
- series of sequenced statements
- concluding statement
- labelled diagrams and flow charts.

Title

Explanations have a title that prepares and leads the reader into the text. This can appear in a variety of forms, from a heading that names the action to a how and why question that is to be answered by the explanation.

General statement

The first paragraph has a general statement that introduces or identifies the scientific or technical phenomenon.

Sequenced statements

The explanation sequence should be made up of a series of happenings or actions that are the focus of the explanation text type. This chain of actions or events creates the phenomenon about which the explanation is written. Generally there is no human involved in the process of events in an explanation. It is important that in addition to researching the facts, pupils understand the reasons behind the facts. Attention should be focused on writing these reasons in their explanations.

The logically sequenced paragraphs explain why or how something happens rather than focusing on an object. It is important that pupils realise that they will need to make thoughtful decisions about what to write and the order in which the information should be presented. Sequences often develop by explaining how the events happen over a period of time. First this happens and then this is followed by the next event. Events may be related according to time, cause or through both. The events should be detailed and accurate and ensure that all elements have been included in the sequence.

Concluding statement

An optional concluding statement can tie up the explanation.

Labelled diagrams

Labelled diagrams and flow charts can be used to clarify information or to add additional information not included in the explanation. In particular, in scientific texts accurate diagrams and illustrations are important to support the text. Pupils will need to research the topic, making notes, drawing diagrams and pictures. They can make use of the scaffolds and outlines to assist with the development of these skills.

LANGUAGE FEATURES OF EXPLANATION TEXTS

- Use of present tense.
- Use of action verbs to describe the events that a subject undergoes,
  e.g. transfers, jumps.
- Use of connectives to link time sequences in a cause and effect sequence,
  e.g. first, then, after, finally, so, as a consequence.
- Use of technical terms,
  e.g. the water cycle, the digestion of food.
- Use of adverbial phrases.
- Use of general nouns,
  e.g. dogs, men.
- Use of abstract nouns,
  e.g. heat.
- Use of pronouns for words already introduced in the text.
- Use of complex noun groups to describe the phenomenon.
  e.g. the flowing river, a spider falls into the family of arachnids.
- Usually, the subject is not human,
  e.g. mountains, rain.
- Use of passive voice,
  e.g. earth is moved, food is divided.
- Use of conjunctions to sequence the event and to keep the text flowing.

Sample annotated text

Ask Professor Know How!

Why does the bathroom mirror mist up when you have a shower?

Why question

Series of sequenced actions

The air we breathe is made up of **oxygen**, **hydrogen** and water vapour (tiny droplets).

The hot **water** coming out of the shower heats the surrounding **air** temperature.

The warmer the surrounding air, the more water vapour **it** can hold. **When** the air **is holding** a large amount of water vapour it appears **as a mist** or fog.

As this mist **touches the cooler surface of a bathroom mirror** the water vapour changes back from a gas to a liquid (**condensation**).

Concluding statement

These are the drops of water you see on your bathroom mirror.

Use of present tense

Use of technical language, e.g. oxygen, hydrogen, condensation

Use of word families, word chains to build information, e.g. oxygen, hydrogen

Use of general nouns, e.g. water, air

Use of pronouns for words already used in the text, e.g. it

Use of conjunctions, e.g. when

Use of adverbial phrases telling how the water vapour appears, e.g. as a mist

Use of connectives to link time sequences, e.g. as

Use of action verbs, e.g. is holding, touches

Use of noun groups, e.g. the cooler surface of a bathroom mirror

Ask Professor Know How!

Why does the bathroom mirror mist up when you have a shower?

The air we breathe is made up of oxygen, hydrogen and water vapour (tiny droplets).

The hot water coming out of the shower heats the surrounding air temperature.

The warmer the surrounding air, the more water vapour it can hold. When the air is holding a large amount of water vapour it appears as a mist or fog.

As this mist touches the cooler surface of a bathroom mirror the water vapour changes back from a gas to a liquid (condensation).

These are the drops of water you see on your bathroom mirror.

Let's talk about it!

Read the explanation 'Ask Professor Know How' with a partner. Discuss what has been explained. Have you noticed this happening in your bathroom? Share experiences. Are there other occasions when you have noticed a liquid changing into a gas, or a gas turning into a liquid? (HINT: it usually involves temperature, heat and a cold source.) Write an example or two below.

_____

_____

_____

_____

Technical terminology

Explanation texts usually use technical terms. Find the scientific words in this explanation. Write them on the lines below.

_____

_____

_____

_____

In the space below, create a glossary for the technical words. (HINT! A glossary lists and defines the words in alphabetical order.)

Tell them why

Name _____

Imagine that you have been asked to explain to younger pupils why the bathroom mirror mists up when you have a shower.

Work with a partner to prepare a short, spoken explanation of this scientific process. Consider using a variety of speech patterns such as emphasis, pitch, pausing and intonation, as well as body language and gestures. Visual information will also be helpful in getting your message across to younger children. You will need to clearly mark all these ideas on your script.

Use another sheet of paper to draft and edit your work, then write the final script on the lines below.

_____

_____

_____

_____

_____

_____

_____

_____

_____

_____

_____

_____

_____

_____

_____

_____

How Are Tornadoes Formed?

Sarah: Do you know what a tornado is?

Ben: Isn't it like a whirlwind?

Sarah: Yeah. It says here that they start in thunder clouds. They're formed in warm, damp air when winds hurl into each other from different directions. In this way it makes a funnel of clouds.

Ben: I saw one on television once … it did look just like a funnel.

Sarah: Well, air gets sucked into this funnel of clouds and it spins really fast. Then it causes lots of damage. When the funnel touches the ground, the tornado turns dark because it swirls all the dirt, dust and everything else high into the sky.

Ben: It sounds a bit like the hose of a vacuum cleaner picking up things.

Sarah: Yeah, but this vacuum can be hundreds of metres high and can race around at something like 500 kilometres per hour.

Ben: Do they keep on moving for ever?

Sarah: It says they last from fifteen minutes to five hours. But imagine how far they'd travel in that time and how much damage they'd cause.

Ben: I wonder what makes them stop.

Sarah: I guess the funnel gets clogged up with dirt, dust and everything so that it can't suck anything else up. When this happens, the cloud gets lighter and gets thinner and thinner and finally disappears altogether.

Ben: It's amazing when you think about it. It's just air moving really quickly that causes all the damage.

Just the facts

Name _____

Sarah has found an interesting book about weather. In this conversation, she explains to Ben what causes a tornado. The explanation is made up of a series of statements about tornadoes. Find these statements and write them on the lines below.

_____

_____

_____

_____

_____

_____

_____

_____

_____

_____

_____

_____

_____

_____

_____

A picture is worth a thousand words

Illustrations or diagrams can make an explanation easier to understand. On another sheet create a series of diagrams to explain how tornadoes are formed. Don't forget to label your diagrams!

Do you know how to....?

Name _____

What else would you like explained about the weather? Think of a list of 'how' or 'why' questions that you could research. Write them on the lines.

_____

_____

_____

_____

_____

_____

_____

Choose one of your questions and research to find the answer. Use rough paper to make your notes and draft your explanation. Write your final explanation in the space below.

ANY QUESTIONS ?

CAN YOU THINK OF SOME QUESTIONS FOR ME, PLEASE ?

How do we breathe?

Name _____

Use these diagrams as a basis, and read at least one other resource, to draft an explanation. Remember to write a general statement to introduce the subject and then explain the sequenced stages before ending with a concluding statement. Draft an explanation on scrap paper, edit and then write below.

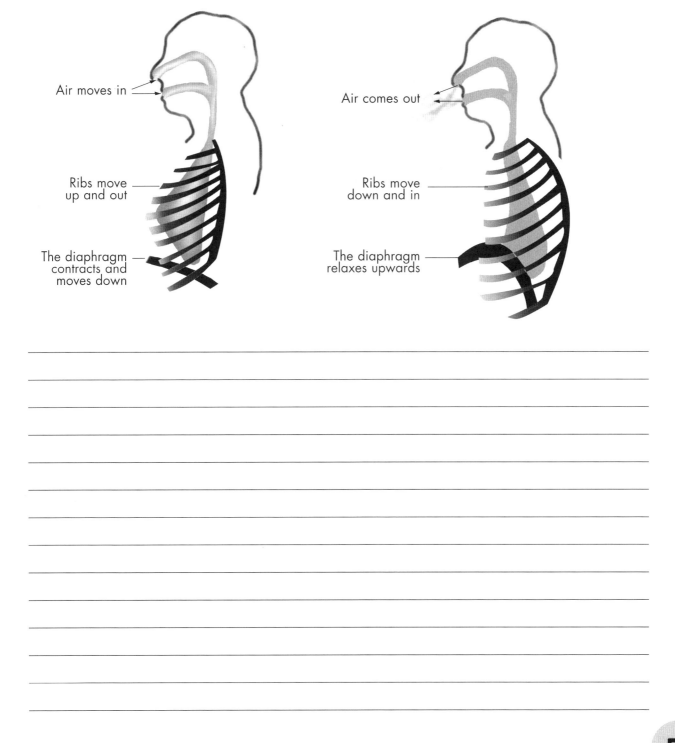

Air moves in

Ribs move
up and out

The diaphragm
contracts and
moves down

Air comes out

Ribs move
down and in

The diaphragm
relaxes upwards

_____
_____
_____
_____
_____
_____
_____
_____
_____
_____
_____
_____
_____
_____

Fax Facts

Fax is a colloquial word for facsimile, meaning a copy or reproduction. Fax machines send and receive printed words or pictures along ordinary telephone lines.

A fax machine is needed at both the sending and receiving end. First, the piece of paper with the message to be sent is fed into the sending machine and the number of the receiving fax machine is dialled.

Inside the fax machine are motorised rollers which then pull the paper over a scanner. When this scanner tracks along each line of the paper, it detects the patterns of light and dark which make up the pictures or words. These patterns are then coded into electrical signals.

These electrical signals are sent down the telephone line to the receiving machine. The receiving machine then decodes the signals back into the same patterns of light and dark. Now the message only needs to be printed.

An electrical current passes line by line over the special heat sensitive paper. When the machine detects a dark pattern it causes an electrical current to pass through the paper. The heat caused by this electrical current turns the paper black. In this way the patterns are converted back into print.

Finally, the paper with the printed message is pushed out of the machine by the receiving machine's rollers. The message has been received!

What's an explanation?

Name _____

With a partner discuss the features of this piece of writing which identify it as an explanation. Write as many of the features as you can in the space below.

_____

_____

_____

_____

_____

_____

_____

_____

_____

_____

_____

WHAT'S AN EXPLANATION, SALLY ?

I KNOW — BUT IT'S HARD TO EXPLAIN .

Find the verb

Reread the explanation and find verbs to fill the table.

VERBS	PAST TENSE	PRESENT TENSE	FUTURE TENSE
Doing *or* action			
Saying *or* asking			
Thinking *or* feeling			
Being *or* having			

Research the facts

Name _____

In the space below write a list of all the different types of communication that you can think of.

_____

_____

_____

_____

Choose one of these to research.

List the key words that you can use as the basis of your search for information.

_____

_____

_____

In the space below write a list of all the places where you think you will be able to find information.

_____

_____

_____

_____

_____

Draw a labelled diagram or a flow chart showing how your mode of communication works.

Concept map

Name _____

Use this concept map to brainstorm a topic of your choice.

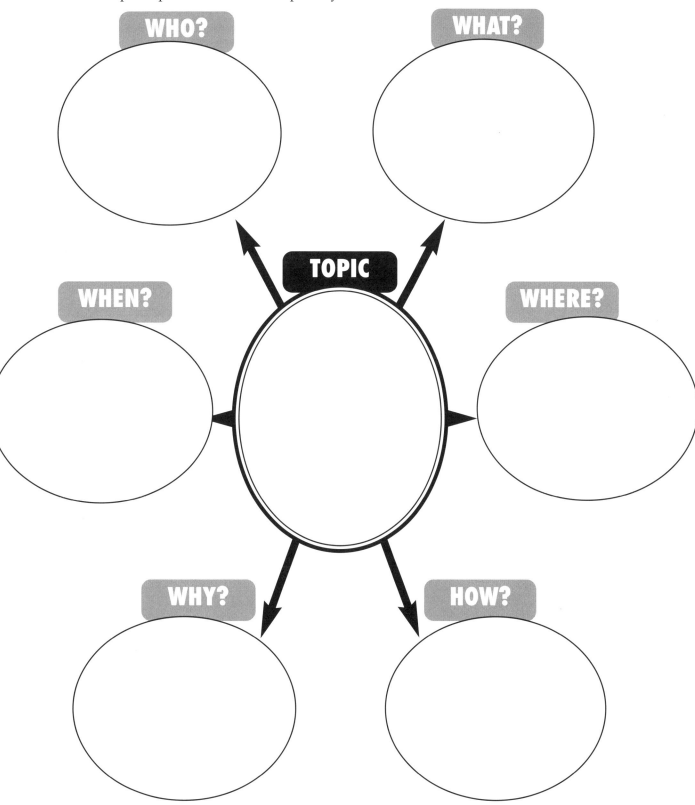

Life Cycle

Research a life cycle of a plant or animal. Draw or write the life cycle in the diagram below.

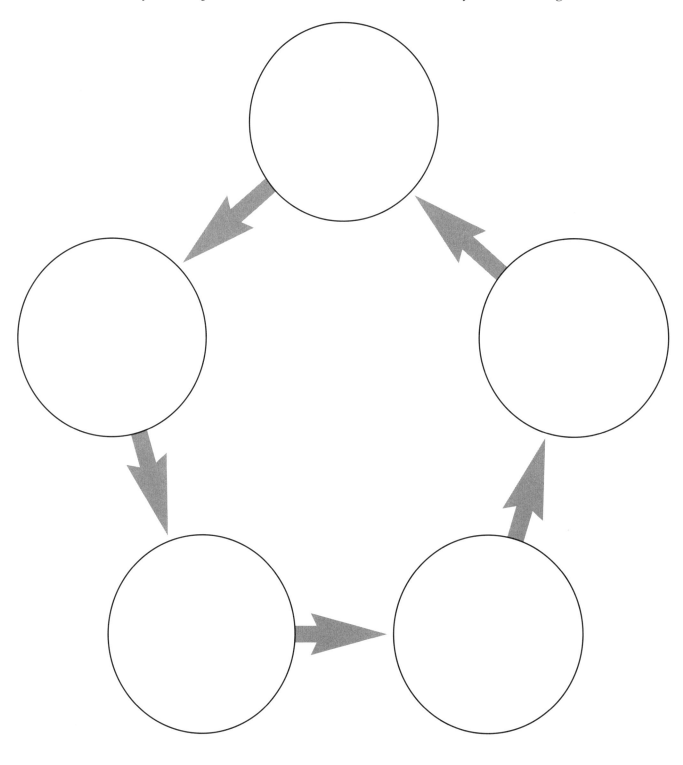

Flow Chart

Name _____

Use the flow chart to create a summary of an explanation you have researched.

Title _____

Explanation scaffold

Name

Use this sheet to plan an explanation on a topic you have researched.

Title
A 'how' or 'why' question.

Introduction
A general statement introducing the subject.

Sequenced statements
Describe the actions in the order that they happen.

Concluding statement
End the explanation by describing how the subject will continue or explaining very briefly what has happened.

Resources
List author, title and publisher of any resources used.

Explanation skills checklist

Name:				
Class:	Date/Level	Date/Level	Date/Level	Date/Level
PURPOSE				
Demonstrates an understanding of the purpose of an explanation.				
STRUCTURE				
Uses a 'how' and 'why' question as a title and focus.				
Writes a clear opening sentence.				
Writes the explanation in a logical sequence.				
Writes a concluding statement.				
Uses diagrams, illustrations, flow charts.				
Includes sufficient information to enable the explanation to be easily followed.				
Recognises different types of explanations.				
TEXT ORGANISATION				
Plans for the writing of explanations.				
Writes general statements or definitions introducing the reader to the subject.				
Sequences all the events in the correct order.				
Writes a clear explanation.				
Shows knowledge of the field and evidence of some research.				
Uses clear visuals that contribute to the understanding of the text.				
LANGUAGE FEATURES				
Writes in the present tense.				
Uses words to show cause and effect.				
Uses conjunctions to sequence events.				
Uses technical words to explain phenomena.				
Uses action verbs.				
Edits and proofreads the draft.				

LEVEL CODES   1 Consistently evident   2 Sometimes evident   3 Not evident

Persuasion texts

Structure and features of persuasion texts

PURPOSE

A persuasion persuades a reader or listener by presenting one side of an argument. By taking a point of view and justifying it, we aim to convince others to see only that side of an issue.

TYPES OF PERSUASION

Persuasions analyse, interpret and evaluate the environment surrounding us. There are a number of persuasion texts which vary according to whether they analyse, interpret or evaluate.

In a persuasion text the audience is being persuaded to a particular point of view. This may be persuading someone to act in a certain way, or justifying an action. Pupils need to develop the skills to recognise that something is one-sided or biased and see that it presents only one point of view, especially if they are being convinced to behave in a certain way, to buy something or to do something.

When pupils are talking they frequently will state a position while making a point. They may then elaborate on it before repeating it. It is important that pupils have a great deal of practice role-playing orally before writing a persuasion.

There are different types of persuasion texts:
- Persuasive writing promotes and sells goods, services and activities; for example, in advertisements and posters persuasive language is used to convince people to do or believe particular things. It has a positive emphasis or bias and is directed at a specific audience. Media advertisements are generally eye-catching with catchy slogans and tunes. This draws people in and makes them identify with the messages and images portrayed.
- Persuasive writing can change the attitude people have or their point of view by putting forward an argument about a specific issue, for example newspaper editorials, political or campaign speeches, letters to the editor, legal defences, debates or sermons.
- Persuasive writing can plead a case, for example *Saving Water*.

Pupils are exposed to persuasive writing every day when they discuss with others what to buy or ask others to suggest what novels to read. Hopefully as pupils develop their skills they will become aware that facts can be interpreted in different ways and that a variety of opinions on an issue may be valid.

Experiencing persuasive writing helps develop a pupil's critical thinking and clarity of expression while they respond to an issue. It encourages pupils to question, research and respond to an argument in a clear, logical way.

STRUCTURE OF PERSUASION TEXTS

Persuasion texts generally begin with an introductory statement of position giving the author's opinion or point of view. This previews the argument that will follow. The next section has a series of logical arguments that convince the audience why this position has been taken. A conclusion ties it all together by reinforcing or summarising the author's point of view.

Statement of position

This is often supported by some background information about the issue in question. The stand taken by the writer may preview in summary form the arguments to be presented. Pupils need to focus on developing a strong statement of position. They can ask themselves the following questions:

- Who am I trying to persuade?
- What am I trying to persuade them to think or do?

- What type of arguments will best catch their attention?
- The statement should be hard hitting and clearly state the position so there is no doubt in the audience's mind.

Argument stage

A number of points are generally made in this section. The number of arguments is flexible and varies in each persuasion. Arguments need to be logically developed and supported and justified with evidence. This justification or elaboration needs to be as effective as possible and take the form of being supported by facts, examples, statistics, tables, visual images, quotes or evidence. All points should relate back to the statement of position. Vague terms, such as the general public, or a large group, should be used with care as the accuracy of these observations needs to be assessed.

The arguments are ordered according to whether the writer believes they are persuasive or weaker arguments. The writer may wish to start with the strongest argument, linking the others. An alternative way is to start with the weaker and build with each argument to the strongest, or they may wish to intersperse the strong arguments with those that are weaker. It is important that each elaboration consists of a number of sentences.

Reinforcement of the statement of position

This is where the argument is emphasised. The summing up of the position in the light of the argument that has been presented reinforces the statement of position and often calls for some type of action on the part of the audience.

Pupils need to focus on reinforcing their statement of position and emphasising their main points by varying their voice, tone, volume, pace, body language and gesture in oral presentations, to persuade their audience.

LANGUAGE FEATURES OF PERSUASION TEXTS

- Word families of general nouns are used, e.g. traffic, people, lights.
- Cause and effect are expressed through conjunctions.
  e.g. because, therefore, so.
- Abstract nouns, such as bravery and horror, and technical words, such as endangered creatures, are used. The issue becomes more scientific from the voice of the expert.
- Action, saying, mental and thinking verbs are used,
  e.g. rescue, challenge, planning, hope.
- Connectives associated with reasoning are used,
  e.g. therefore, so, because, the first reason.
- Emotive words are used,
  e.g. ugly, cunning, burglar.
- Evaluative language is found,
  e.g. It is most important that all people...
- The personal pronoun I is often removed. The author speaks persuasively of people, places and things already in the text,
  e.g. she, them.
- Reported speech is used to refer to what the majority of people have said on the issue.
- Generally, the text is written in the present tense but may change to past tense for historical evidence or future tense if predictions are being made.
- Frequent use of passive voice to structure the text,
  e.g. Fear has been expressed that...
- A degree of certainty is found in the words selected,
  e.g. often, nearly, most, generally, might, could.

Sample annotated text

Saving Water— We Must All Play Our Part

TEXT ORGANISATION ↓

LANGUAGE FEATURES ↓

Lucy is concerned about the amount of water people use. Here is the speech she presented to her class.

TIME'S UP!

Use of present tense, e.g. is, think

Use of word families to build information, e.g. water, dams, streams

Use of modal verbs, e.g. should

Statement of position

I **think** everyone **should** understand the importance of saving **water**. Water **is our most valuable resource**. It **gives** life to all living things, including us, and many people continue to waste it.

Use of action verbs, e.g. gives, dried up

Series of logical arguments with strongest argument first, followed by its elaboration

Firstly, streams and dams in farming areas in some parts of the world have almost dried up completely. Crops are ruined and dead cattle and sheep dot the landscape. Farmers are **suffering** dreadfully. They are living in **poverty** and extreme debt.

Use of evaluative language, e.g. so desperately, our most valuable resource

Use of connectives to sequence arguments, e.g. firstly, secondly

Argument and elaboration

Secondly, many people don't even have enough water to drink, cook or wash with. Saved water could be transported out to the inland towns and communities that need it **so desperately**.

Use of cause and effect, e.g. streams have dried up ... crops ruined and cattle dead

Death is certain for some of our native flora and fauna. Rivers, and **streams** can no longer provide life-giving water.

Use of abstract nouns, e.g. death, poverty

Argument and elaboration

Another reason is that our waterways are becoming too overloaded and polluted. **Water is wasted** on washing cars, watering lawns and having long showers and deep baths. It then drains into the sewage system, dumping soapy and polluted water into the sea.

Use of passive voice, e.g. Death is certain for our flora and fauna

Calls of action on the part of the audience

As of today don't leave the tap running while you brush your teeth. Hide the garden hose **and** insist Dad washes the car on the lawn (tell him the car doesn't need a wash anyway). You must limit all family members to 3-minute showers **and** buy the bathroom a water saving shower nozzle for an early Christmas present. Write letters immediately to both your local council and member of parliament telling them that laws restricting wasteful use of water **must** be passed.

Use of emotive language, e.g. suffering, water is wasted

Use of conjunctions, e.g. and

Use of degree of certainty in selected words, e.g. certain, are ruined, must

Reinforcement of statement of position

We **must** save water and we must do it now!

Saving Water – We Must All Play Our Part

Lucy is concerned about the amount of water people use. Here is the speech she presented to her class.

I think everyone should understand the importance of saving water. Water is our most valuable resource. It gives life to all living things, including us, and many people continue to waste it.

Firstly, streams and dams in farming areas in some parts of the world have almost dried up completely. Crops are ruined and dead cattle and sheep dot the landscape. Farmers are suffering dreadfully. They are living in poverty and extreme debt.

Secondly, many people don't even have enough water to drink, cook or wash with. Saved water could be transported to the communities that need it so desperately.

Death is certain for flora and fauna. Rivers and streams can no longer provide life-giving water.

Another reason is that our waterways are becoming too overloaded and polluted. Water is wasted on washing cars, watering lawns and having long showers and deep baths. It then drains into the sewage system, dumping soapy and polluted water into the sea.

As of today don't leave the tap running while you brush your teeth. Hide the garden hose and insist Dad washes the car on the lawn (tell him the car doesn't need a wash anyway). You must limit all family members to 3-minute showers and buy the bathroom a water saving shower nozzle for an early Christmas present. Write letters immediately to both your local council and member of parliament telling them that laws restricting wasteful use of water must be passed.

We must save water and we must do it now!

List the arguments

Name _____

Read 'Saving Water'. What is the message that Lucy wants to get across to her listeners? Reread the speech with a partner and write your response below.

_____

_____

_____

Lucy supports her opinion by listing arguments to provide evidence that she is right. List her arguments below.

1 _____

_____

2 _____

_____

3 _____

_____

4 _____

_____

Lucy asks the audience to help too. She has made some suggestions. Can you find and list them?

Lucy's suggestions:

_____

_____

_____

_____

_____

Talk about it with a partner. What other suggestions can you think of?

My suggestions:

_____

_____

_____

_____

Write a letter

Lucy suggests we write a letter to the local council or a member of parliament. So, let's do it! Use some of the arguments you found in the text and add some new arguments of your own. Write a draft copy. Use the space below to write your edited version. Don't forget to use a letter format showing address, date, greeting and signing off.

Ban the Bikes

10 September 2005

Dear Sir,

For quite a while now I have been very concerned about the number of children in our area who persistently continue to ride their bikes in Bargaintown Shopping Centre.

Firstly, I would like to say I find this behaviour dangerous. Shoppers are in danger of being knocked over. Much of the population in this area is elderly and does not have the physical energy to dodge speeding, swerving bikes.

I can't see why they need to ride through the middle of a busy shopping centre. The leisure park is only two blocks away. There would be more space for them to practise their fancy manoeuvres without sending overladen shoppers scrabbling for cover.

In addition, it is not only dangerous for shoppers but also for the bike riders themselves. They too are in danger of taking a nasty spill.

Bike riding on footpaths and other pedestrian areas is illegal. I, and many of your readers, are at the stage of appealing to the police to patrol these areas.

Finally, I'd like to know what the parents of these children think. Do they know where they are riding their bikes? Parents seem to have very little control over their children these days.

A decision to ban bike riding in the Bargaintown Shopping Centre will provide a safer environment for us all. I urge all shoppers to lodge a complaint immediately with the council.

Yours faithfully

Helen Smith

Letter to the Editor

Name _____

Read the 'Ban the Bikes' letter. Now it's your turn. Write a letter to the editor either supporting the letter, or arguing against it.

Include an opening statement of position, statements supporting why you feel this way and a final statement summing up your position or suggesting an action.

Draft your letter. Check that you have words to persuade the audience and that your arguments make sense. Write it in the space below, using your neatest handwriting.

_____

_____

_____

_____

_____

_____

_____

_____

_____

_____

_____

_____

_____

_____

ARE YOU TIRED OF THE SAME OLD MUESLI BARS?

Then it's time you crunched

WUNDABARS

WUNDABAR

Scientifically proven to increase the energy levels of athletes during strenuous exercise.

ALL NATURAL INGREDIENTS

TASTES GREAT

- High in complex carbohydrates
- High in natural fibre
- Low in sugar
- Low in fat

Enjoy as a snack or before and after exercise

One won't be enough!

Let's talk about it

Read the 'Wundabars Advert'. Work in a group of three or four friends to discuss the advertisement. Who is it aimed at? What is it trying to persuade them to do?

_____

_____

What features has the writer used to make the advertisement more persuasive? List as many as you can.

_____

_____

_____

_____

Sing a jingle!

Still in your group, compose a jingle to advertise Wundabars. Write it on the lines below, then perform it for the class.

_____

_____

_____

Word dash

How many synonyms for these words can you find? Think of as many as you can, and then check in a thesaurus to find more.

strenuous	natural	increase	complex

Assert yourself

Name _____

One won't be enough! How many ways can you rewrite that statement to make it more or less probable that one won't be enough? Here is one idea; think of at least five more.

One might not be enough.

❑ _____

❑ _____

❑ _____

❑ _____

❑ _____

Now, rank the statements in order from the most persuasive (1) to the least (5) by writing a number in each box.

Words that sell

What kinds of words sell or persuade? Look through some old newspapers or magazines and find some examples. Copy or paste them in the space below.

A new product is launched

Name _____

Write a magazine advertisement for a new product. You will need to consider:

your product

your audience

how you can best persuade your audience to buy your product.

Plan and draft your advertisement here, then make a neat copy on art paper.

Research grid

Name _____

Think of three arguments and research different opinions on them using the grid below.

Questions	1	2	3
Interviewees' names	Response	Response	Response

Persuasion scaffold

Name _____

Use this sheet to write a persuasive piece on a topic of your choice.

INTRODUCTION

The author presents a point of view of the argument.
A question or emotional statement can be used to gain audience attention.

_____
_____
_____
_____
_____

SERIES OF ARGUMENTS TO CONVINCE THE AUDIENCE

Each paragraph begins with a topic sentence that introduces a new argument.
Details follow, supporting the argument.
Emotive words persuade the audience into believing the author.

_____
_____
_____
_____
_____
_____
_____
_____
_____
_____
_____
_____
_____
_____

CONCLUSION TO SUM UP THE ARGUMENTS

The author restates his or her point of view.
A summary of the above facts can be included here.

_____
_____
_____

Persuasive writing

Name _____

Self-assessment e.g. How do you rate yourself as a writer of persuasive arguments?

```
[blank box]
```

Range and preferences e.g. What type of audience is easiest to write for? How do you make your writing clear and interesting?

```
[blank box]
```

Skills e.g. How do you plan your persuasive texts? Do you research to support arguments? In the reinforcement of position, is the stand clearly summarised? How do you edit your work?

```
[blank box]
```

Current projects e.g. What are you writing now? What would you like to write?

```
[blank box]
```

Persuasion skills checklist

Name:				
Class:	Date/Level	Date/Level	Date/Level	Date/Level
PURPOSE				
Understands the purpose of persuasive texts.				
STRUCTURE				
Clearly states a problem in the introduction.				
Writes a strong statement of position.				
Supports the opening statement with background information.				
Formulates an argument, selecting facts to support and elaborate a point of view.				
Uses a variety of strategies to persuade the audience and reinforce the position.				
Identifies different forms of persuasive writing.				
TEXT ORGANISATION				
Understands the function of each stage.				
Develops a well-sequenced plan.				
Organises each point and its elaboration into appropriate paragraphs.				
Sequences points from most effective to least effective.				
Can locate and research relevant information.				
Able to detect contradictory evidence.				
LANGUAGE FEATURES				
Aware of the needs of the audience.				
Uses conjunctions to link cause and effect.				
Differentiates between fact and opinion.				
Uses emotive words.				
Uses degree of certainty in words selected.				
Uses evaluative language.				
Uses abstract and technical words appropriately.				
Uses reported speech to refer to expert comments and research.				
Writes in the present tense and changes to past or future when appropriate.				

LEVEL CODES   1 Consistently evident   2 Sometimes evident   3 Not evident

Discussion texts

Structure and features of discussion texts

PURPOSE

A discussion presents differing opinions, viewpoints or perspectives on an issue, enabling the reader to explore different ideas before making an informed decision.

TYPES OF DISCUSSION

Experiencing discussion texts helps pupils to think clearly and critically. It encourages pupils to listen and respond to others' opinions, to ask pertinent questions and to present an argument in a clear and coherent way. It helps pupils become aware that facts can be interpreted in different ways and that a variety of opinions on an issue may be valid.

Throughout their lives pupils will need to make decisions. Rather than simply responding emotively, it is important that they develop the skills to look at both sides of an argument objectively before making a rational decision. This text type will give pupils the opportunity to develop the skills of finding information to support their arguments and emphasises the importance of anticipating arguments and responding to these.

Discussion texts are concerned with the analysis, interpretation and evaluation of issues. In effective discussion, all points of view on an issue are considered and attitudes change when different perspectives are seen.

Informal discussions should initially involve pupils in decision making and problem solving processes. Pupils should begin by discussing areas that require no research so that they are encouraged to express a point of view. It is important, and will help their understanding, if they are given situations to discuss where there are many different points of view, for example ask the class to discuss the positives and negatives of keeping a kitten that a child has found on the pavement. Pupils can take on differing roles of the child who found the kitten, the parent of the child, the original owner of the kitten and a sibling who is allergic to cats. This will broaden their thinking and make them aware that the same situation can be viewed from different perspectives.

In this text type pupils begin to explore areas that are unfamiliar to them. The writing involves research, interviewing and surveying of involved participants to find their point of view. Written discussions should have their points supported by personal experience, survey results, interviews and research. Discussion texts can be found in editorials, newspaper articles, trial judgements, phone-in radio, and survey results. When reading discussions, pupils need to focus on persuasive evaluative words used by authors to influence the reader.

Pupils can write discussions on different topics. In Geography, for example, discussions can be written exploring the issue: Should more high-rise buildings be allowed in the local shopping centre? In Science pupils can discuss: Should fossil fuels be our choice of energy in the future? In PSHE a possible issue could be: Should sport be compulsory for all primary school pupils?

Discussions provide opportunities for developing the use of many language skills. In oral sessions pupils can work towards developing their ability to factually justify a point or support an opinion. They will have to search for supporting evidence and critically discuss the arguments of others. Characters in novels also have to make decisions or are offered alternatives. This gives pupils the opportunity to explore different perspectives and build an understanding of discussion. Pupils need to develop their ability to involve and persuade an audience while evaluating the strength of different arguments.

Techniques used in discussion texts include: thought provoking questions, analysis of points of view and repetition of words, phrases and concepts.

STRUCTURE OF DISCUSSION TEXTS

There are four stages in a discussion:
- a statement of position supplying necessary background information
- arguments for and supporting evidence
- arguments against and supporting evidence
- a recommendation or conclusion.

Statement of position

A discussion begins with a brief introduction describing the situation. This introduction recognises that there are two points of view.

Arguments for and supporting evidence

The next few paragraphs elaborate the arguments for the issue, based on researching, surveying or interviewing people.

Arguments against and supporting evidence

The next set of paragraphs describes the arguments against the issue, based on researching, surveying or interviewing people.

Each paragraph should be clearly structured with a topic sentence supported by details. The supporting material could be reported speech reflecting comments, specialists who have responded to the issue, or supporting evidence from research or surveys. Thinking and action verbs are used to persuasively establish and evaluate each argument.

Recommendation or conclusion

The discussion ends by presenting a personal point of view before concluding. The recommendation or conclusion sometimes sums up both sides of the argument if they are fairly balanced, or can recommend one argument over the other if the evidence is overwhelming.

LANGUAGE FEATURES OF DISCUSSION TEXTS

- Use of general nouns to make statements,
  e.g. machines, cars.
- Use of relating verbs,
  e.g. is.
- Use of thinking verbs that express a personal point of view,
  e.g. consider, contemplate.
- Use of connectives to link arguments.
  e.g. on the other hand, however, in the same way.
- Use of conjunctions to link clauses.
- Use of detailed noun groups.
- Use of varying degrees of certainty (modality),
  e.g. perhaps, probably, should, might.
- Use of adverbs of manner,
  e.g. honestly, rapidly.
- Use of abstract and technical terminology.
- Use of saying verbs to quote.
- Use of quoted and reported speech.
  e.g. Mr White, when interviewed, said...
- Use of factual adjectives,
  e.g. my *recent* adventure.
- Use of adjectives expressing an opinion,
  e.g. my *horrifying* adventure.
- Use of comparative adjectives,
  e.g significant, more significant, most significant.
- Use of evaluative language.
- Use of the present tense.

Homework...Who Wants It? (part 1)

A class held a debate. Here is the transcript.

Topic: Homework should be compulsory, every day, for all pupils in the school.

Pupil 1 (agree)

I think homework is really important in primary school because kids need to get into good habits with homework so that when they get to senior school they know how to work at home and it doesn't come as a big shock to them.

Pupil 2 (disagree)

I agree that it's important to get into good homework habits but I think that compulsory homework every day is too much. Children need to spend time doing other things like playing sports, learning how to play musical instruments or just reading for pleasure.

Pupil 3 (unsure)

I believe that a little bit of homework is OK although not every night and not at the expense of other activities like exercise. And I also don't know what 'compulsory' means. Does it mean that pupils will be punished if they don't do their homework? I'm not sure about the exact meaning of the sentence we're debating so I can't say whether I agree with it or not.

Homework...Who Wants It? (part 2)

Pupil 4 (agree)

I don't think we spend enough time at school to learn all we need to learn so we should do some of the work at home and besides, if it's not compulsory people won't do it. Also, sometimes it's really noisy at school and you can't concentrate well enough to do a good job on something. You can concentrate better at home. Homework is also good for finishing things that you didn't get time to finish at school.

Pupil 5 (disagree)

I don't agree with what the previous speaker said about it being quieter at home to get things done. In some homes it's really noisy and therefore impossible to concentrate. So some kids would have trouble with compulsory homework every night. I don't agree that pupils should get homework every night.

Pupil 6 (unsure)

I can't say that I totally agree. I agree that sometimes homework is OK but not compulsory every night.

Pupil 7 (agree)

I think a bit of homework every day is good for everyone. It gets you into good work habits, so I agree with the statement.

Pupil 8 (disagree)

I don't agree with the statement. It's really difficult to be fair with homework. Some teachers give lots of homework and some teachers only give a little bit and also some kids take ages to do what other kids can do really quickly so I think you need to think about each kid individually and it's impossible to say absolutely that homework should be compulsory for everyone.

Pupil 9 (unsure)

I can't agree with the statement that homework should be compulsory every night for all pupils. I think Reception kids are too little to have homework. They need to run around after school. Maybe ten minutes four nights a week is good for year three and by year six, maybe thirty minutes a night five nights a week is OK. But not every night for every kid. That's too much! So I agree a bit but not totally.

Sample annotated text

Homework...
Who Wants It?

Topic: Homework should be compulsory, every day, for all pupils.

TEXT ORGANISATION OF A DEBATE

LANGUAGE FEATURES

Pupil 1 (agree)

I think homework is really important in primary **school** because **kids** need to get into **good** habits with homework so that when they get to senior school they know how to work at home and it doesn't come as a **big** shock to them.

Use of general nouns, e.g. kids, school

Use of adjectives expressing opinion, e.g. good, exact, big

Arguments for and supporting evidence

Pupil 2 (disagree)

I agree that it's important to get into **good** homework habits **but** I **think** that compulsory **homework every day** is too much. Children need to spend time doing other things like playing sports, learning how to play musical instruments or just reading for pleasure.

Use of thinking verbs, e.g. believe, think

Use of noun groups, e.g. homework every day

Arguments against and supporting evidence

Pupil 3 (unsure)

I **believe** that a **little** bit of homework **is** OK **although** not every night and not at the expense of other activities like exercise. And I also don't know what 'compulsory' means. Does it mean that pupils will be punished if they don't do their homework? I'm not sure about the **exact** meaning of the sentence we're debating **so** I can't say whether I agree with it or not.

Use of relating verbs, e.g. is

Use of conjunctions, e.g. so, but, although

Use of varying degrees of certainty, e.g. little, sometimes, impossible

Arguments for and supporting evidence

Pupil 4 (agree)

I don't think we spend enough time at school to learn all we need to learn so we should do some of the work at home and besides, if it's not compulsory people won't do it. Also, **sometimes** it's really noisy at school and you can't concentrate well enough to do a good job on something. You can concentrate better at home. Homework is also good for finishing things that you didn't get time to finish at school.

Arguments against and supporting evidence

Pupil 5 (disagree)

I don't agree with what the previous speaker said about it being quieter at home to get things done. In some homes it's really noisy and therefore **impossible** to concentrate. So some kids would have trouble with **compulsory homework every night**. I don't agree that pupils should get homework every night.

Use of detailed noun groups, e.g. compulsory homework every night

Pupil 6 (unsure)

I can't say that I totally agree. I agree that sometimes homework is OK **but** not compulsory every night.

Arguments for and supporting evidence

Pupil 7 (agree)

I think a bit of homework every day is good for everyone. It gets you into good work habits, so I agree with the statement.

Use of adverbs of manner, e.g. quickly

Arguments against and supporting evidence

Pupil 8 (disagree)

I don't agree with the statement. It's really difficult to be fair with homework. Some teachers give lots of homework and some teachers only give a little bit and also some kids take ages to do what other kids can do really **quickly** so I think you need to think about each kid individually and it's impossible to say absolutely that homework should be compulsory for everyone.

Readers have to reach their own conclusion from arguments that have been presented

Pupil 9 (unsure)

I can't agree with the statement that homework should be compulsory every night for all pupils. I think Reception kids are too little to have homework. They need to run around after school. Maybe ten minutes four nights a week is good for year three and by year six, maybe thirty minutes a night five nights a week is OK. But not every night for every kid. That's too much! So I agree a bit but not totally.

What do you think?

Name _____

Read 'Homework ... Who Wants It?' The purpose of discussion is to explore different opinions about an issue. Verbs are important in discussion texts to show thoughts and feelings. List the verbs that appear in the extract.

_____

_____

Connecting words are also important in a discussion because they link the ideas in a sequence so that the text makes sense. List all the connecting words that appear in the discussion.

_____

_____

Make the connections

Use some of the following connectives to link the sentences below.

> *otherwise, however, in this way, thus, since, because, likewise, similarly, on the other hand, alternatively, whereas*

1. Some people agree with homework. Other people disagree with homework.

_____

2. Some pupils are lucky enough to come from homes where it is possible to get homework done. Some pupils live in homes where it is impossible to complete homework.

_____

_____

3. Some teachers give too much homework. Some teachers don't give any homework.

_____

_____

4. Many parents like their children to get homework. Other parents disagree with homework. They believe it is a waste of time.

_____

_____

5. Some pupils need extra time to finish their work. These pupils benefit from homework. If homework takes too long then it's not fair for the pupil.

_____

_____

Write the discussion

Name

Reread the extract from the 'Homework ... Who Wants It?' debate and then use it to write a discussion. Draft your text on scrap paper first then write it in the scaffold below.

Opening statement to outline the issue	
Arguments in favour of homework	
Arguments against homework	
Concluding statement or recommendation	

YOU'LL NEED TO REORGANISE.

Conducting a survey

Name _____

Work with a partner. Interview pupils and teachers at your school to find out their opinions about homework. Ask them to give reasons for their opinions.

Make a table which tallies the numbers who agree and disagree with homework and their reasons. Draw up your table below then write some conclusions that you can draw from it.

Conclusions:

_____

_____

_____

_____

For and Against

Name _____

Work in groups of six to decide on a topic for a parliamentary debate.
Here are some topic ideas to get you started:

1. Teachers should be forced to retire at age 40.

2. All pupils should board at school for their schooling in years 3–10.

List the opinions for and against your party's view.

FOR the party	AGAINST the party

Debating

Name _____

Decide which three group members will speak for the topic and which three will speak against the topic. Prepare for the debate and then hold the debate in front of the rest of your class or another class at your school.

What were the arguments?

After the debate write the different arguments as a written discussion. You could use the same scaffold as the previous page. Write on scrap paper first and then write your discussion below.

_____

_____

_____

_____

_____

_____

_____

_____

_____

_____

_____

_____

_____

YOU'RE FINALLY OLD ENOUGH TO LEAVE SCHOOL, SIR.

Discussion scaffold

Name

Use this sheet to write a discussion on a topic of your choice.

Statement of position
Introduce the topic and supply necessary background information.

_____

_____

List arguments for the statement and support with evidence

Argument 1 --

Evidence --

Argument 2 --

Evidence --

Argument 3 --

Evidence --

List arguments against the statement and support with evidence

Argument 1 --

Evidence --

Argument 2 --

Evidence --

Argument 3 --

Evidence --

Recommendation or conclusion

_____

_____

_____

Discussion skills checklist

Name:				
Class:	Date/Level	Date/Level	Date/Level	Date/Level
PURPOSE				
Understands the purpose of a discussion.				
STRUCTURE				
Writes a clear statement on an issue, supplying background information.				
Writes arguments for and against an issue.				
Backs up positions with supporting evidence.				
Sums up arguments or recommends one side of the argument over the other.				
Recognises different types of discussions.				
TEXT ORGANISATION				
Develops a well-sequenced plan.				
Locates relevant information.				
Is aware of the reader's needs.				
Organises arguments into appropriate paragraphs.				
Detects contradictory evidence.				
Gauges whether arguments are facts or opinions.				
Concludes by summarising, solving the problem or persuading people to do something.				
LANGUAGE FEATURES				
Uses shared language and technical terminology meaningfully.				
Uses general nouns and detailed noun groups.				
Uses varying degrees of certainty.				
Uses conjunctions and connectives.				
Uses quoted and reported speech to support arguments.				
Writes in the present tense.				

LEVEL CODES   1 Consistently evident   2 Sometimes evident   3 Not evident

Non-fiction text types

Year / Term	Text type/objective	Model texts	Page
Y3T1	Reports T20: to read information passages, and identify main points or gist of text	Sandy Cove	40
Y3T2	Instructions T14: how written instructions are organised, e.g. lists, numbered points, diagrams with arrows, bullet points, keys	Hopscotch	22
Y3T3	Letters T22: experiment with recounting the same event in a variety of ways, e.g. in the form of a story, a letter, a news report	Letter Home	6
Y4T1	Instructions T25: to write clear instructions using conventions learned from reading	Directions	28
	Reports T27: to write a non-chronological report, including the use of organisational devices	Bananas	36
Y4T2	Explanations T25: to write explanations of a process, using conventions identified through reading	Tornadoes	56
Y4T3	Persuasion T18: from examples of persuasive writing, to investigate how style and vocabulary are used to convince the intended reader	Saving Water	71
	Discussion T21: to assemble and sequence points in order to plan the presentation of a point of view, e.g. on hunting, school rules	Homework	86